Politics and the policy development process are routinely seen as a matter of selecting a policy action developed from a set of available options. National Socialist ideology rejected traditional politics and developed an extremist approach to implement its agenda. Hitler and the National Socialist movement provide a clarifying moment in history to the dangers a nation confronts when the "true believers" empowered with an extreme ideology are in charge of governance. The National Socialists created ideological imperatives that restricted debate and winnowed policy options creating inefficiencies and application errors that a broader and more holistic policy approach would have avoided or mitigated. National Socialist ideological imperatives distorted the structures, functions, and priorities of institutions preventing the formation of acceptable war aims and inhibited the nation's ability to fight a protracted war of attrition.

The struggle with National Socialism provides liberal democracy a warning to challenge ideological extremists seeking to capitalize on internal and international crises. Liberal democracies in the struggle to effectively challenge ideological extremists must not dismiss them as irrational. Rather, liberal democracies should learn the ideological extremist' philosophical underpinnings and accept that their policies and actions seek to conform in a rational manner.

After being appointed Chancellor, Adolf Hitler implemented National Socialist ideological preferences around leadership, race, and socioeconomic relations. Hitler's uncompromising will exploited Germany's historic and cultural development to transform his preferences into policy imperatives. The implementation of derived ideological imperatives by supportive lieutenants and military officers had a significantly negative impact on the nation's ability to conduct prolonged modern warfare.

1

Germanic Culture and Völkisch Ideology

Germany, after defeat in World War I, was in political chaos and threatened by social revolution. In this environment the fragile democratic Weimar Republic arose from the ashes of defeated Imperial Germany. The new German polity was strife ridden with a multitude of sociopolitical ideas and movements vying to capture the attention of citizens, elites, veterans, and opportunists. Political competition in the Weimar Republic was characterized by limited sociopolitical support to the emergent democratic civil society and its struggling institutions. Extreme political parties of the left and right actively campaigned for the overthrow of the state and imposition of a revolutionary order. These disaffected groups drew inspiration from German culture and history to formulate their ideology and propagandize the public.

From the extreme right emerged the Nationalsozialistische Deutsche Arbeitspartei (NSDAP), the National Socialist German Workers Party. The National Socialists drew on multiple sources of nationalist information, beliefs, myths, and conspiracies to form their ideology and philosophy or world view, a Weltanschauung. The National Socialist had a right-nationalist racist weltanschauung that involved concepts affecting all aspects of human life and culture while asserting a prescriptive sociopolitical program to advance the nation's aspirations and remedy the ailments of a defeated post-World War I Germany.[1] Hitler's speeches and writings highlight the importance of the National Socialist's right-nationalist racist weltanschauung. Weltanschauung was a frequent theme in *Mein Kampf* with two chapters in the book title: "Weltanschauung and the Party" and "Weltanschauung and Organization."[2] Hitler repeatedly referred to his weltanschauung stemming from a historical process; unlike Marx, he defined the historical process through racial struggle instead of class struggle.

Historian Fritz Stern describes the period from the French Revolution of 1789 and the accompanying Napoleonic Wars to the turmoil after World War I as the time that gave rise to a

Germanic Ideology.[3] This Germanic Ideology rejected the enlightenment and the many sociocultural forces unleashed and adopted by the liberal western European states. In Germany, liberalism was rejected because it was believed to have negative impacts on German culture.[4] Conservatives hated liberalism because it was seen as interfering with the true character of the German völk through the imposition of foreign culture and the creation of institutional barriers within society.[5] The conservative rejection of liberalism attacked the bourgeois life of materialism, parliament and parties, and perceived lack of effective leadership. Conservatives sought a replacement to fill the moral and cultural decay liberalism unleashed. In response to the forces unleashed by the enlightenment the Germanic peoples developed strategies to adapt to modernity that reflected their conservative culture. Germanic ideology sought a new community that was absolutist and expressed a faith in fixed standards, certainty, nationalism, and reestablishing contact with their past.[6]

National Socialism as the Völkisch Movement

A key component to NSDAP ideology was derived from the party members' Germanic understanding of race, ethnicity, and culture. In Germany the rejection of western liberalism was most clearly expressed through its self-identification of the Germanic peoples and their cultural attributes and artifacts. Hitler and the National Socialists were effective at uniting farmers, urban workers, middle class, industrialists, and disaffected elements that otherwise would have conflicting political views around a few core ideological principles that derived from the wider Germanic weltanschauung. By the use of extreme nationalism and racism the National Socialists created coalitions and unified the various groups of the right.[7]

Following Germany's defeat in World War I, the power of völkisch movements could be seen in the organizing of nationalistic paramilitary organizations to protect the nation. In 1919 there was widespread revolutionary instability threatening national unity and traditional social order. In response to territorial pressures in the east and revolution at home free associations of dismissed military units and members backed by business elites formed right wing militias called the Freikorps.[8] The Junker aristocracy and middle class found common cause to defeat the left and the masses of disaffected workers to restore social order. These Freikorps soldiers, using decentralized small unit tactics learned during the war, fought against Polish, Russian and Lithuanian efforts to assert territorial claims against a weakened Germany. Within Germany the Freikorps put down left wing attempts to create socialist republics or worker Soviets in Bavaria, the Ruhr industrial region, and Berlin. When the Freikorps disbanded in 1921 these men continued to seek comradeship within the numerous right wing sociopolitical movements that sprung up after the war. Munich became a center of activity for former Freikorps members. Many joined the National Socialist's uniformed arm the Storm Troopers, Sturmabteilung (SA).[9]

The NSDAP use of völkisch culture appealed to a wide swath of society and was primarily concerned with instituting a social program popularized by Pan-German völkisch beliefs. These beliefs involved extreme nationalism, exclusion of undesirable races from the völk, racial anti-Semitism, paternalism, militarism, and included mystical notions of a Teutonic past that formed a Germanic Culture based on order, harmony, and hierarchy.[10] Economically the National Socialists trumpeted a return to traditional class relationships as the means to develop the nation. The socialist character in their program was centered on the proper social relations that were in need of restoration to support industry and labor. The party believed the nation would prosper once proper social relationships were implemented between the classes of laborer and capitalist.[11]

National Socialism propagandized two obstacles to the restoration of German honor, power, and prestige. The first obstacle to German greatness was the terms imposed on Germany after World War I. They were seen as morally unjust, designed to keep Germany from her rightful great power position, and keeping the völk enslaved to the international financiers, the

Jews, of the victorious western allies. The National Socialists extreme racism identified the Jew as the primary obstacle to German national revival and greatness. They identified the Jews as a transnational people working in concert to manipulate the gentiles for their own ends. This racial weltanschauung gave German's understanding for the cause of World War I, Germany's military defeat, the revolution of November 1918, and the chaos of the Weimar Republic.[12]

The NSDAP program of 1920 survived largely unchanged for twenty-five eventful years. During this period the party experienced rapid growth from a fringe group on the extreme right to acceptance as a mainstream national party suitable for coalition governance. Its growth and political acceptance was remarkable. It survived a ban after the failed putsch of 1923 to be re-established by Hitler upon his release from Landsberg Prison in 1924. The stability of the party and its program during this period is a reflection of Hitler's faith in himself and opportunistic personality.[13] The re-established party was under pressure from within to change the program in support of a class-based approach to gaining power. The ideological crises created a leadership struggle that led to Hitler's dominance of the party, a shift to electoral politics, and the emergence of a Hitler personality cult. With the shift to electoral politics Hitler refused to allow internal conflict over the meaning of the party program. While insisting that the program was unchangeable and correct in its form the party shifted from a programmatic emphasis to one of general themes focused on principles to be interpreted and realized under the central leadership of the leader, führer.

Rejection of a programmatic emphasis allowed Hitler to capitalize on his rhetorical skills and the party's skillfully cynical use of propaganda.[14] Hitler replaced the programmatic message with a nationalist race-based appeal to the public, as opposed to a Marxist class-based message. Because of his political charisma and oratory skill Hitler could provide emphasis or adapt any aspect of the party program to meet the needs of the moment or audience; thereby allowing the party to be all things to all men.[15] The electoral message of Hitler was centered on leadership, race, and socioeconomic relations. The populist appeal of the nationalist message was summed up in the slogan Ein Völk, Ein Reich, Ein Führer. One People, One Nation, One Leader provided strong mental imagery that sanitized the least favorable aspects of the National Socialist interpretations of leadership, race, and socioeconomic relations.

National Socialism and Leadership

The leadership principle, Führerprinzip, is a central component to understand National Socialist ideology, structure, and function after Hitler's release from prison. The party believed the führerprinzip was the ideal model of leadership and was the basis for the formal and informal workings of the party and state organizations. The führerprinzip significantly explains the wider ideological implications of governmental policy choices, the workings of the bureaucracy, and the culpability of senior civilian and military leaders for the national security decisions made about strategy and operations. In *Mein Kampf* Hitler expressed his theory on the relationship between leaders and followers:

> They never understood that the strength of a political party lies by no means in the greatest possible independent intellect of the individual members, but rather in the disciplined obedience with which its members follow the intellectual leadership. The decisive factor is the leadership itself.[16]

Hitler explains that two military groups in competition will draw strength from the inherent leadership and discipline qualities of their group. The triumphant group will not be the one who seeks to train their members broadly in strategy; but rather, is the group that has the most superior leadership combined with the most disciplined, blindly obedient, best drilled troops.[17]

Explicit in Hitler's thinking on leadership was the superiority of a high quality, ideologically imbued leadership cadre as opposed to a large general purpose apolitical leadership force. By the acceptance of the Führerprinzip the party and state were instruments, the means, to

6

accomplish Hitler's goals.[18] Eberhard Jäckel, in his examination of Hitler's philosophy, sums up

the centrality of Hitler's leadership to the structure and functioning of the state:

> There was only one Führer, extremely isolated even on the human level, and there were his extensions, appointed by him either directly or indirectly, on the various levels of the power structure. On the administration level, this resulted eventually in a complex system of chanceries – each with a presidential, governmental, Party, and military function – which on the one hand passed along to the Führer all matters requiring his decision, and on the other hand formulated and handed down the so-called Führer-decisions, which were frequently oral. This entire system was based on a concept of absolute and hence obedience which comes closest to the concept of following orders as it prevails in the military, from where it was probably derived. Everyone swore allegiance to Hitler's own person, not to the state.[19]

A well-documented element concerning this leadership philosophy was the lack of

knowledge by even his key lieutenants about the Führer's upcoming plans let alone the intent of

long term goals.[20] This information vacuum allowed the development of rival power centers

within the party and the state and at times required the direct and immediate attention by the

Führer. The most threatening leadership conflict to the stability of the regime came to a climax in

1934 with the extra-legal purge of the SA. Ernst Röhm wanted his 4.5 million SA to assume the

leadership role of defending the revolution and the state rather than the Wehrmacht. Hitler

fearing a Wehrmacht or SA coup purged the SA. The purge killed hundreds of political rivals and

ended a serious leadership challenge to Hitler while securing the everlasting loyalty of the

Wehrmacht. The officer corps and conservative elites believed their interests were aligned with

Hitler and ignored the unlawful nature of the purge and regime's growing criminality.

National Socialism and Race

Racism was a central component of the National Socialist weltanschauung linking anti-

Semitic myths with the practical problems and concerns of the völk. The party exploited

Germanic Ideology and economic insecurity of the middle class to gain power and to justify anti-

Semitic policies that exploited racial schisms in society. Hitler said, "There is only one possible kind of revolution. It is not economic or political or social, but racial."[21] The national

community's health, Volksgemeinschaft, rested on maintaining the purity of the völk's blood and

race. It was the state's responsibility to protect the national community and through this create

true national socialism that would transcend all aspects of national life; economic, political, and

social.[22] Hitler's belief in the importance of racial purity was also a rationale to explain German

failures of the past while justifying racial policy.

In *Mein Kampf* Hitler describes Jews as the originators and bearers of internationalism,

democracy, and pacifism and that this racial group sought to impose their sociopolitical

dominance by challenging the racial interests of the Aryan peoples. The National Socialist

weltanschauung on nationalism, führerprinzip, and heroism or militarism was in a racial struggle

with Jewish internationalism, democracy, and pacifism. Hitler claimed the Jewish belief in

internationalism, democracy, and pacifism weakens the Aryans existing race value, destroys its

personality value, and paralyzes its natural strength for self-preservation.[23] Hitler further

comments on the importance of the racial struggle and the consequence of failure:

> If at the beginning of the War and during the War twelve or fifteen thousand of these
> Hebrew corrupters of the people had been held under poison gas, as happened to hundreds
> of thousands of our very best German workers in the field, the sacrifice of millions at the
> front would not have been in vain. On the contrary: twelve thousand scoundrels eliminated
> in time might have saved the lives of a million real Germans, valuable for the future.[24]

These comments sought to reinforce the stab in the back myth, to build racial awareness,

and create resistance to the existing sociopolitical order. It is well documented the message of

racial struggle greatly helped the party in electoral politics, implement racial discrimination, and

justify mass murder.[25] Additionally, this quote expressed the belief that sociocultural impacts of

war on domestic Germanic populace provided a political rational, opportunity, and a necessary

pre-condition to racially purify the nation.

National Socialism's Socioeconomic Relations

The National Socialist understanding of economics significantly impacted policies surrounding the nation's economic recovery. National Socialist's viewed Jewish social, political, and economic activity in the private and public sphere as alien to the national community and a significant and preventing the corrective remedy proposed by the party to install völkisch principles of governance.[26] German Jews were seen as part of an international conspiracy that sought to deprive ethnic Germans of their völkisch principles, liberties, and rights. National Socialists claimed international Jewry used both Marxist and liberal economic theory to gain dominance of the international order.

National Socialist's expressed a proper adjustment of domestic and international socioeconomic relations as vital to establish a proper völkisch relationship among the classes and reduce liberal bourgeois influence. In order to liberate the German economy from foreign influence and support rearmament the National Socialists had an economic policy of agrarianism and autarky. The belief that the economy was a means to state power and state power was the means to National Socialist ideological goals drove the party to seek economic nationalism over international trade. The government sought to discourage international trade and emphasize economic self-sufficiency through a balance between supply and demand. Autarky would secure the liberty of the state, freedom of action within foreign policy, and independence in times of emergency.[27] This meant that economic policy was subordinate to foreign policy and as such was a means to an ends. As such, seen through National Socialist ideological imperatives economic policy was designed to support the means of power.[28] The concept of racial struggle was supported by Hitler's assertion that in the urge to preserve the species in its efforts to form communities the state is a national organism and not an economic organism.[29] The Volksstaat, popular state, and social policy was to bring about a welding together of the völk to prepare it for war and expansion.[30]

National Socialism Ideology, Imperatives, and Effects on Strategy

Hitler's writings and speeches document a clear preference to see strategic options, decisions, problems, and threats through a military lens. Time and again he speaks of "blood and steel" as the preferred manner to resolve Germany's international problems. The military option provided a decisive way to impose a solution on rival races and nations. Hitler's militancy and desire to dominate the military professionals required him to consolidate power over the Armed Forces High Command, Oberkommando der Wehrmacht (OKW) and institute OKWs rise over the Army High Command, Oberkommando der Heeres (OKH). Hitler's consolidation of power over OKW and OKH allowed him to dominate strategic and operational concerns that were typically the preview of the OKH General Staff and army field commanders. The führerprinzip was adapted to the relationships between civilian-military leadership and had a corrosive effect on rational strategy formulation and operational design regarding war, economics, and command that narrowed options available.[31]

National Socialist ideology had negative effects on Germany's national command structure and functioning in determining and executing strategy. The führerprinzip was grafted onto a modern bureaucracy and as such was ill suited to a nuanced national security policy formulation process. In fact, in accordance to Hitler's narrow strategic formulations, options were deliberately narrowed; and yet, once strategy was determined its coherence and effectiveness was further limited due to the Third Reich's Byzantium complex system of chanceries each with a presidential, governmental, party, and military function.[32]

Numerous examples exist of the Third Reich's failure to holistically consider the diplomatic, informational, economic, and military application of national power on available strategic options.[33] This failure is seen in the rearmament of the Wehrmacht and the militarization of foreign policy. Rearmament presented domestic and international problems for Germany and was challenged by limited raw materials, manpower shortages, consumer demand requirements, deficits, lack of coherence, and persistent inter-service rivalry. These problems were surmountable only because Hitler intended a strategy to rearm not in depth but in breath to provide limited military capabilities suitable for an aggressive foreign policy and the conduct of small localized wars.[34] The long term impact of rearmament in defiance of the Versailles Treaty and an aggressive foreign policy narrowed the strategic options by the consolidation of an international opposition to German interests and a militarized response by the other great powers.

Hitler's aggressive foreign policy supported with a credible military capability allowed him to assert German interests and gain early diplomatic victories that tipped the balance of power in Europe in Germany's favor. These diplomatic victories had a significant impact on strategy and future options available to Germany and the other great powers. For example, the German occupation of the remainder of Czechoslovakia in April 1938 in violation of the Munich Agreement showed a clear great power response. This move altered decades of British policy of maintaining a small professional army when it introduced conscription and increased the regular army from 4 to 16 divisions and authorized 16 Territorial Divisions in reserve.[35] Diplomatically Britain hardened it stance to German claims against Poland and sought to create a coalition of powers to oppose Germany militarily.

A critical requirement for any state interacting within the international security environment is to make risk assessments. The führerprinzip allowed Hitler to operate on the international stage with limited domestic oversight to the risks he was posing to the nation. Albert Speer assessed him as an intelligent amateur unburdened by conceptions of standards and practices to approach problems in strategy and operational planning. Speer associates Hitler's ignorance of the prevailing "rules" of the geopolitical game as the source of his victories in the early years of international conflict and war. Hitler's autocratic personality, combined with a perceptive if untrained intelligence, was able to take advantage of adversaries trained to apply the rules in a "rational" manner. Hitler's intelligent opportunism allowed him to achieve surprise time and again over adversaries. Unfortunately for Hitler his ignorance of the rules in periods of military setbacks revealed his incompetence in catastrophic ways.[36]

A review of Hitler's foreign policy formulations developed in the 1920s and documented in the diplomatic and military history of the Third Reich shows a consistency of ideological principles on strategy that centered on the reversal of the Treaty of Versailles and the requirement to gain territories in the east.[37] In *Mein Kampf* and *The Second Book* Hitler expressed his foreign policy goals as developing in three phases. In the first phase Germany would undergo internal consolidation, rearmament, and develop alliances with Great Britain and Italy to isolate France. In the second phase France would be defeated and removed as a source of military challenge to Germany's future ambitions. In the third and final phase a war for conquest of lebensraum and world power dominance would be undertaken against the Soviet Union.[38]

Hitler detailed a couple ways to achieve his goals through either an Anglo-German or a USSR-German alliance to challenge the strategic and military situation in Europe. He preferred an Anglo-German alliance to give Germany the freedom to challenge French military power on the continent. Under this preferred formula, following a French defeat a victorious Germany would seize lebensraum from the racially inferior and weak Jewish-Bolshevik state while leaving the British Empire alone and unchallenged at sea. The least preferred USSR-German alliance formula would seek after the defeat of France colonies and a naval and trading empire overseas in direct conflict and Great Britain. Hitler saw the ways available to achieve the goals in his phased approach as flexible and open to capitalizing on opportunity.

The strategic formulation combined with the actual events, characters, and capabilities of the international system in the late 1930's reflects remarkably well a consistent and rationally opportunistic approach by Hitler to further foreign policy goals. After the fall of France in 1940 it was important to Hitler to develop a strategic formula that allowed for the protracted war with Great Britain to continue while maintaining the strategic initiative on the continent. The ideological imperative of conquering lebensraum with its promise of vast human and material resources to support a continued war with Great Britain and prepare for possible war with the U.S. was viewed as a sound strategy by Hitler and his colleagues consistent with their weltanschauung of geopolitics and racial struggle. Hitler adapted his strategic formula and decided to invade the Soviet Union and gain lebensraum sooner rather than later. Hitler believed Great Britain's military defeats made it unable to challenge Germany on the continent for some time to come giving him a window of opportunity to conquer the Soviet Union.

The ideological dimensions of the military campaigns fought were fully realized in the war against the Soviet Union. It was planned, organized, and implemented as a War of Annihilation, a Vernichtungskrieg, against the Soviet Union and manifested Hitler's view of a implementing an ethnic struggle, a Volkstumskampf, on a grand scale supported by the technological and the bureaucratic efficiency of the modern industrial state.[39] The National Socialist military strategy merged their ideological racism and the traditional nationalist goal of empire in the east.[40] The ethnic struggle within a war of annihilation was believed the historical unfolding of the struggle for life or death of peoples and races not of social-economic groups and would determine who would gain supremacy and control of the vast resources, territory, and peoples of the east [41] Final victory would be absolute attaining international dominance and imposing a Pax-Germanica on the world. The Pax-Germanica would be a National Socialist ideological victory with defeat of racial inferiors, conquest of national territory sufficient to secure natural resources, and colonial expansion.[42]

National Socialism Ideology, Imperatives, and Effects on Operations

Operation *Barbarossa*, was the first campaign planned and executed under the operational approach called Blitzkrieg. Previous operations against Poland, Norway, and France were operational designs akin to those used in the closing months of World War I. These campaigns revealed operational and tactical capabilities that were only somewhat understood at the start of the war and refined during the war. By 1941 the Germans believed they developed a superior and economical method of making war, but the swift victories in the first two years of the war masked significant operational deficiencies stemming from National Socialist ideology. Hitler's decision to seek final victory through conquest of the Soviet Union had a significant impact on military capabilities. The expanded war into the Soviet Union provides useful insights revealing the limitations of the National Socialist ideological imperatives of leadership, race, and socioeconomic relations on operations. The strategic goal of defeating the Soviet Union required the National Socialist government and military to economically balance ends, ways and means in an attempt to support Blitzkrieg operations in the Soviet Union.

The German government and military viewed National Socialist leadership as the decisive capability and once committed to war with the Soviet Union sought to leverage this advantages to win operational victories against an inferior cultural, social, and racial opponent. This belief had an effect in the relationship between the national civilian and military leadership. Hitler progressively imposed changes to the culture of the Wehrmacht and the army in particular. The General Staff entered into its relationship with Hitler agreeing that another war was inevitable and the only way to reverse the Treaty of Versailles and regain Germany's rightful place in Europe.[43] There was a tension between the army and Hitler in the development of strategy and the conduct of operations during the war. The tension revealed the General Staff's belief that in any future conflict it was the group best suited to make decisions on military strategy and operations.[44] The General Staff's historic role in strategy and operations ran counter to Hitler's expressed desire to be the sole arbiter of determining war aims and the hierarchal relationships he was willing to tolerate from military subordinates in discussing strategy and operations.

Hitler's leadership role expanded in ways the state and military could not anticipate. On the death of President Paul von Hindenburg in 1934 Hitler assumed the powers of armed forces commander-in-chief. In 1938 Hitler supplanted the Minister of War as de facto commander-in-chief (OKW). In 1941 Hitler named himself commander-in-chief of the German Army (OKH) and for a time commander Army Group B in its drive to the Caucuses on the eastern front.[45] Hitler's desire to maintain authority and control made him unable to effectively delegate power to subordinates. He falsely believed that his expanded powers allowed him to impose his will on all situations resulting in greater effective efforts by his subordinates. Hitler's illusion of control repeatedly frustrated his efforts resulting in ever greater efforts made to effect control.

Hitler's desire for expanded control of theater level operations and specific named operations led him to eventually assign all theaters except the eastern front to OKW. The creation of OKW theaters of war led to the decline of OKH's ability to see the whole strategic picture and knowledgably adjust theater level army assets to meet operational requirements. The General Staff was denied its traditional ability to conduct a strategic review and provide guidance to coordinate all German army operations in multiple theaters. Additionally, OKH and the General Staff had to provide much needed planning personnel, intelligence, logistic, and operational support directly to the understaffed and undertrained OKW organization. The ideological imperative of the führerprinzip facilitated by the technical and procedural capabilities of the OKW / OKH Command and Control Systems supplanted the mission-oriented command system with an order-oriented system.[46] Additionally, the order-oriented command structure guaranteed a situation where lines of command, authority, and control were confusing and a source of biased reporting back to the Führer[47]

Hitler's position as the Führer made him indispensable to the running of the government and resolving process problems and conflicts. Hitler's central power position, limited expertise in critical fields, and temperament combined to create institutional conflict, inefficiencies, wastage, and poor policy choices. Albert Speer in his memoirs relates numerous episodes where Hitler was required to make critical armament decisions that had significant second and third order effects on operational capabilities of the Wehrmacht. Speer notes Hitler's lack of understanding in the need to supply the armies with a sufficient quantity of spare parts. In early 1942, prior to the start of the second summer campaign, it was explained to Hitler by General Heinz Guderian, the Inspector General of Tank Ordnance, that a reduction of new tank production by 20 percent was required to ensure an adequate level of parts to quickly repair the existing tanks in service. Hitler rejected this economical and operationally sound recommendation in favor of new vehicles that would also quickly suffer from lack of proper maintenance.[48]

Operational Marginalization of OKH

Hitler's use of the OKW command structure and marginalization of the army's General Staff greatly reduced effective planning and execution of operations. This reduction in General Staff influence and the convergence of Hitler as the principal military-economic-diplomatic-political-ideological leader created a situation that allowed and even encouraged access by party functionaries to the internal planning and conduct of military operations. This trend led to a reduction of the army's influence in forming, training, and equipping new units available to fight the war and weakened the army's traditional right as the nation's principal protector. When Germany confronted operational setbacks the government sought to redress the tactical and operational difficulties by ensuring the political and ideological reliability of the Wehrmacht. The army, as the principal service, and its General Staff were most threatened by the Führer's lack of confidence in the Wehrmacht commitment to National Socialist goals. Other services and National Socialist functionaries were able to take advantage of the army's diminished role in military affairs and assert their own interests. To remain politically relevant the army adopted National Socialist ideology to doctrine and leadership training.

By comparison the Luftwaffe and its Commander in Chief Reichsmarschall Herman Goring were viewed as being ideological reliable. In September 1942 Reichsmarschall Goring in response to a personnel crisis to replace army casualties on the Eastern Front volunteered to free up excess personnel to support the manpower requirements. Goring was able to politically promote his service by insisting that the Luftwaffe retain control of the personnel and that they be formed into Luftwaffe field divisions rather than transfer these desperately needed men to the reserve army for training and replacement into the front line divisions. The Luftwaffe organized these forces and employed them with little success and it was not until November of 1943 that the Luftwaffe Divisions were transferred to the army.[49]

Another challenge to the army was the growth of the Waffen-SS within the Wehrmacht to ensure a politically and ideological reliable force committed with the proper zeal to fight the struggle with Bolshevism.[50] The Waffen-SS divisions achieved a higher level of motorization and mechanization than their army counterparts and by 1943 the Waffen-SS represented five percent of the Wehrmacht's fighting strength of 9,730,000 and more than more than twenty-five percent of its panzer divisions.[51] The Waffen-SS growth did affect the resources available to the army to maintain its military capabilities.

Hitler's Völkisch Operational Bias

Unity of effort in war is a prerequisite for effective planning, organization, and conduct of military operations. The working relationships between the party, state and military bureaucracy, Hitler, and his civilian and military leaders were deficient and often after cross-purposes in support of war aims. The result was further wastage, inefficient use of human and material resources, and loss of operational focus. The German government and military viewed Blitzkrieg as a decisive and economical capability generated and supported by its effective balance of ends, ways and means. To support the operational approach of Blitzkrieg the General Staff drew upon the theory of Total War learned from its experience in World War I. Total War would target all sources of enemy strength, not just its military forces, to quickly end the war. Therefore, resources of the nation would be economically managed to produce operational capabilities to fight under an authoritarian government complying with the General Staffs military supremacy.[52]

Hitler and many of his party lieutenants viewed Total War as the escalation of the continuing racial struggle started before the war. During the war the racial struggle took on an importance and urgency demanding its resolution as a German triumph. This triumph was ideologically necessary to punish the Jews for perceived cultural, historical and racial attacks on the völk and for the Jewish-Bolshevik conspiracy that expanded the struggle into a world war of national survival. Victory in the racial struggle would address the social-ideological threat of international Jewish-Bolshevism, reorder the racial environment of Europe with the Aryan finally ascendant over the untermenschen, and secure the material and human resources Germany required to maintain her as the dominant power. The racial struggle as a major component of Total War prevailed and was made a national effort involving all the hierarchies of the German government, the Wehrmacht, industry, and the party.[53] Franz Halder, Chief of the General Staff, reports in his diary on March 30th 1941 a meeting between the Führer and his generals in which he explains war aims and the nature of the war to be conducted against Bolshevik Russia. Halder reports the future war as a clash between two ideologies when he reports Hitler's remarks as:

> Crushing denunciation of Bolshevism, identified with social criminality. Communism is an enormous danger for our future. We must forget the concept of comradeship between soldiers. A Communist in no comrade before or after the battle. This is a war of extermination. If we do not grasp this, we shall beat the enemy, but thirty years later we shall again have to fight the Communist foe. We do not wage war to preserve the enemy. Extermination of the Bolshevik commissars and the Communist intelligentsia.[54]

Halder notes in his diary that the OKH operation order for *Barbarossa* needed to embody the coming war with Bolshevik Russia as very different from the war in the west and that in the east harshness today means lenience in the future.[55] These rationalizations by a leading German general ten weeks prior to the start of operations against the Soviet Union reflect on the broad acceptance and support given to meet the will of their Führer. Halder sought moral solace as a member of an elite group able and willing to do the difficult and messy task required of the nation when he says, "Commanders must make the sacrifice of overcoming their personnel scruples."[56]

Hitler's concept of Total War as a racial vernichtungskrieg imposed operational limitations on the Wehrmacht while accepting strategic objectives beyond the capability of Germany's war economy. The tension surrounding allocating finite national ways and means significantly effected Germany's operations once the war became global. Hitler's successful dominance of the political-military sphere and his ideologically rigid approach to operations in an effort to ensure total victory was ultimately undermined by an unwillingness to rapidly and decisively adjust his ideological goals to the economy of total war. Hitler made a calculated choice and accepted the risk to under resource the means necessary to fight a global war of attrition. Hitler did this because he believed in the superiority of National Socialist leadership and the operational approach of Blitzkrieg to win economical wars of rapid decision fought successively against ill prepared and operationally outmoded enemies.

Operational Opportunity Costs

It is clear that imposed ideological imperatives affected the material and personnel resources available to the war economy. Rearmament was given a priority by the National Socialist Party and the Wehrmacht so that by 1936 the army was implementing a four year program to create a force of 102 divisions with 2.6 million men able to conduct offensive warfare. To support the army's plan Hitler created an economic program called the Four Year Plan under the supervision of Goring. The Four Year Plan called for rearmament to be an industrial priority regardless of the economic consequences.[57] This rearmament plan was sufficient to prepare Germany by 1939 to fight limited sequentially separate wars of duration, scale, and purpose against ill prepared and geographically constrained enemies. This was not the case when Hitler embarked on a new war with the Soviet Union.

Hitler's made the political and strategic calculus to maintain a limited war economy by selectively targeting resources for the critical military capabilities most needed at the time. Hitler believed that Operation *Barbarossa* would provide a quick and complete victory over the Soviet Union making available vast resources to the war economy while simultaneously limiting the wars impact on the availability of consumer goods to the people. This approach resulted in a fundamental failure to match or adjust the ways and means of the state to meet the strategic goals and operational capabilities required of the Wehrmacht in this new war.

The Wehrmacht's operational capabilities expanded and matured and by 1941 were significantly enhanced reflecting the pride and strength of successful combat operations, but Hitler's ideological desire to maintain a limited war economy as Germany prepared forces to invade the Soviet Union reflected a lack of strategic vision. Under this weak economic footing the decision to invade the geographically expansive, densely populated, industrially strong, militarily capable, and ideologically united Soviet Union demonstrated a fundamental failure to balance the risks of initial operational failure with sound economic, political, and military preparations prior to the invasion of the Soviet Union. Many civil and military experts believed the resources were not sufficient to generate the military means sufficient to conduct a rapid campaign of maneuver over the vast distances and poor infrastructure of the Soviet Union. Many military sources conclude that the Wehrmacht of 1941 to execute Blitzkrieg was only suited for operations in fair weather over good roads.[58] The combination of tracked and motorized vehicles of all sorts meant that only 20 percent of the Wehrmacht's forces were capable of the mobility necessary to reach the envisioned strategic objectives.[59]

Ideological imperatives had significant impacts on the character of the strategy, operational design developed, and unfolding events in the campaign. The strategic concept and operational plan developed and executed by OKW and OKH for the invasion of the Soviet Union relied on the key assumption that the Blitzkrieg would provide operational success to end the new war in one campaign season. It called for the combined armed forces to conduct a series of rapid and decisive attacks in the western Soviet Union to defeat the Red Army in detail west of the Dnieper River; thereby, freeing the Wehrmacht, supported by allies, to capture key cultural, political and economic objectives. Military planners believed it vitally important to secure these key objectives prior to the Red Army's regeneration of forces or shifting of strategic reserves. After accomplishing the operational objectives, Germany would establish a defensive line generally along the Ural mountain range separating Asiatic Russia from European Russia.[60]

The campaign plan failed to exploit anti-Russian feelings of the peoples of Central and Eastern Europe because German racial concerns for the future conquered lands of the east colored how they saw the potential help of the local inhabitants. The German racial view was that the inhabitants in the conquered lands were to be subject peoples and not potential collaborators against Russian imperialism. Hitler's refusal to adjust his war aims from a German-Soviet war fought to meet German national security-ideological interests to a broader European war of liberation for East European ethnic groups desiring national survival against the International Communist menace missed a potential source of German military strength. This failure to exploit the interest of the oppressed and exploited Soviet citizens was an opportunity cost that assisted in the defeat of Germany. The National Socialist failure to exploit long standing Ukrainian grievances to fight Soviet Communism was one of many opportunities missed by the Germans to mobilize local resources. The Ukrainian Nationalist Movement (UPA) was an anti-Soviet organization forming the second largest partisan bands operating in the eastern front. These Ukrainian bands fought Russian Communist bands and even Red Army units behind Soviet lines when the Red Army liberated territory from the Wehrmacht. The UPA asked to collaborate with the Wehrmacht and sought a German general to assist in organization and tactical leadership of the Ukrainian partisan bands. Unfortunately for the German war effort Hitler continuously refused to sanction these requests.[61]

German racial motivations affected the war economy and wasted resources and capabilities that could have been utilized to fight the war. The Schutzstaffel (SS) growth reflected a direct challenge to the army for resources and a unified war effort. The SS created a vast economic, police, military, and intelligence empire that reached into and affected all aspects of the German war economy, military operations, and security operations.[62] To commit industrial level genocide the German state had to commit vast resources to build six large industrial killing centers, 1,634 concentration camps and their satellites and more than 900 labor camps.[63] The SS disregarded physical and military obstacles in their fanatical efforts to fulfill the Führer's will to destroy racial enemies, especially the Jews, of the Third Reich. Rationalists who opposed these disruptions were expected to make accommodations. Hitler's Total War ideology against the untermenschen occupied scores of thousands of military personnel and often paralyzed the railway system, even during critical battles. Many Jewish war workers were motivated to avoid the killing centers sought to make themselves as indispensable to the war effort as possible making them a reliable and focused labor pool. Jewish motivations were not enough to overcome the racial policies of the Holocaust which resulted in the killing of 3 million productive workers, many of them highly skilled.[64]

Operational Interference Disrupts Blitzkrieg

On July 16 the city of Smolensk's fell to the most successful German field army with Moscow only a further 200 miles distant. Hitler assessed that this presented a critical operational decision point since the Wehrmacht reached the Dnieper River without having destroyed the Red Army. The clearest and most significant operational interference by Hitler during the war ensured the failure of Blitzkrieg in 1941. The negative effect of the führerprinzip was Hitler's insistence, against the best military advice by his top field commanders, to attack divergent objectives to secure periphery goals.

On September 5, while the Wehrmacht was engrossed in the Battle of Kiev, Hitler directed the seizure of Moscow at the earliest date. On September 26 the panzer units were released back to the central army group to prepare for the attack on Moscow and on October 2 the army group launched Operation Typhoon and encountered initial success despite the first snow fall on October 7. In the first two weeks the Wehrmacht encircled two Soviet Armies between Vyazma and Bryansk capturing 650,000 prisoners, 5,000 guns, and 1,200 tanks. By October 20 the converging armor pincers were within forty miles of Moscow.[65] The October rains and the early arrival of winter severely affected the Wehrmacht's mobility and slowed its tempo. By December 5 along the entire Eastern Front the Wehrmacht was a spent force in exposed forward positions attempting to transition to the defense. This force had to confront the Red Army counter attack on December 6th. This interference resulted in Germany no longer fighting a war of maneuver but rather a war of attrition.

National Security and Ideological Imperatives

The multiple National Socialist ideological imperatives effecting strategy and operations ensured the failure of Germany to defeat the Red Army in the opening gambit of its vernichtungskrieg against the Soviet Union. This failure meant that Germany was locked into a volkstumskampf that consumed enormous resources and would be protracted over years rather than months. National Socialist ideology surrounding leadership, race, and socioeconomics created policy imperatives that missed and/or winnowed options available to the German state in developing strategy and operational designs in fighting World War II. The defeat outside Moscow was a culmination of converging ideological imperatives in the realm of politics, leadership, strategy, economics, and operations that trapped the Germans into a war of attrition without having prepared the economy, people, and military psychologically and materially to support such a requirement.

This analysis provides a cautionary reminder of the inherent conflicts that arises when national leadership places ideological imperatives before sound strategic and operational requirements. Liberal democracies must resist the desire to dismiss ideological extremists as irrational and must allow that extremist' policy preferences and actions seek to conform in a rational manner to their philosophy. The acceptance of rationality on behalf of ideological extremists assists liberal democracies to identify and develop strategies to confront them in a forthright and realistic manner. Additionally, liberal democracies need to foster diverse sources of knowledge and opinion in the national security debate to guard against a tendency for political factions to lobby policies seeking conformity to a liberal democratic ideological worldview resistant to sociological, economic, geopolitical, and military reality.

[1] Ideology definition. ("Encyclopedia Britannica Company Merriam-Webster" 2012)

[2] Eberhard Jäckel, *Hitler's Weltanschauung: A Blueprint for Power.* Translated by Herbert Arnold. (Middleton, Conn.: Wesleyan University Press), 13.

[3] Fritz Stern, The Politics of Cultural Despair: A Study in the Rise off the Germanic Ideology, (Berkeley and Los Angeles, CA: University of California Press, Ltd., 1989), xii-xiii.

[4] Ibid.

[5] Ibid.

[6] Ibid.

[7] Jackson J Spielvogel, *Second Edition, Hitler and NAZI Germany, A History.* (Englewood Cliffs, NJ: Simon & Shuster Company), 49-50.

[8] James Taylor and Warren Shaw, *Dictionary of The Third Reich.* (New York, NY: Penguin Books, 1997), 99.

[9] Ibid.

[10] Ian Kershaw, *Hitler 1889-1936 Hubris.* (New York, NY: W.W. Norton and Company, 2000), 135.

[11] Spielvogel, *Second Edition, Hitler and NAZI Germany, A History,* 97.

[12] Ibid., 28.

[13] Ibid., 41.

[14] Kershaw, *Hitler 1889-1936 Hubris,* 253.

[15] H.W. Koch, Introduction to Part I. *Aspects of the Third Reich.* Edited by H.W. Koch. (Hong Kong: MacMillan), 7.

[16] Adolf Hitler, *Mein Kampf.* Translated by Ralph Manheim. (Boston, Mass: Houghton Mifflin Company), 457.

[17] Ibid.

[18] Jäckel, *Hitler's Weltanschauung: A Blueprint for Power,* 82.

[19] Ibid.

[20] Ibid.

[21] John Weiss, *Ideology of Death: Why The Holocaust Happened In Germany.* (Chicago, IL: Elephant Paperbacks, 1997), 271.

[22] Ian Kershaw, *Hitler 1889-1936 Hubris,* 137.

[23] Jäckel, *Hitler's Weltanschauung: A Blueprint for Power,* 98-99.

[24] Hitler, *Mein Kampf,* 679.

[25] There are multiple sources that reference National Socialist's assertion that the International Jew deserved racial discrimination and murder. Kershaw's *Hitler 1889-1936 Hubris,* John Weiss' *Ideology of Death: Why The Holocaust Happened In Germany,* Ayçoberry, *The Social History of the Third Reich 1933-1945* and Hitler's books *Mein Kampf* and *The Second Book* offer documentation.

[26] Pierre Ayçoberry, *The Social History of the Third Reich 1933-1945.* Translated from French by Janet Lloyd. (New York, NY: The New Press), 49-58.

[27] Jäckel, *Hitler's Weltanschauung: A Blueprint for Power,* 78.

[28] Hitler, *Mein Kampf,* 150.

[29] Ibid., 151.

[30] Jäckel, *Hitler's Weltanschauung: A Blueprint for Power,* 80.

[31] Geoffrey P Megargee, *Inside Hitler's High Command,* (Lawrence, KS: United Press of Kansas, 2000), XV.

[32] Jäckel, *Hitler's Weltanschauung: A Blueprint for Power,* 82.

[33] *Document On German Foreign Policy 1918-1945, Series D 1937-1945 The War Years,* (Washington D.C.: United States Government Printing Office), Vol. XII, No. 650.

[34] Burton H. Klein, "German's Economic Preparations for War". *Aspects of the Third Reich.* Edited by H.W. Koch. (Hong Kong: MacMillan), 361-364.

[35] Murray Williamson and Allen R. Millett, "Armored Warfare: The British, French and German Experiences," in *Military Innovation in the Interwar Period,* eds. Williamson Murray and Allan R. Millett (Cambridge: Cambridge University Press, 1996), 11-12.

[36] Albert Speer, *Inside the Third Reich,* Translated by Richard and Clara Winston, Introduced by Eugene Davidson. (New York and Toronto: Macmillan), 275.

[37] Jäckel, *Hitler's Weltanschauung: A Blueprint for Power,* 37-43.

[38] Ibid., 39.

[39] Alexander B. Rossino, *Blitzkrieg, Ideology, and Atrocity: Hitler Strikes Poland.* (Lawrence, KS: University Press of Kansas), xiv.

[40] Ibid.

[41] Jäckel, *Hitler's Weltanschauung: A Blueprint for Power,* 88.

[42] Jürgen E Förster, *Military Effectiveness Volume 3 The Second World War*, New Edition. Edited by Allan R. Millett and Williamson Murray. (New York, NY: Cambridge University Press, 2010), 181.

[43] Megargee, *Inside Hitler's High Command*, 12.

[44] Ibid., 11.

[45] Earl F. Ziemke, *Military Effectiveness Volume 3 The Second World War*, New Edition. Edited by Allan R. Millett and Williamson Murray. (New York, NY: Cambridge University Press, 2010), 280.

[46] Förster, *Military Effectiveness Volume 3 The Second World War*, 210.

[47] Richard L. DiNardo, *Germany and the Axis Powers, From Coalition to Collapse.* (Lawrence, KS: University Press of Kansas), 195.

[48] Speer, *Inside the Third Reich,* 280.

[49] Förster, *Military Effectiveness Volume 3 The Second World War*, 190.

[50] Ibid., 189.

[51] Ian Baxter, *SS: The Secret Archives, Eastern Front.* (London, England: Amber Brooks Ltd), 64.

[52] Megargee, *Inside Hitler's High Command*, 14.

[53] Paul A Johnson, *A History of the Jews.* (New York, NY: Harper and Row Publishers), 496.

[54] Franz Halder, *The Halder War Diary 1939-1942.* Abridged edition of the English translation of: Kriegstagebuch. Edited by Charles Burdick and Hans-Adolf Jacobsen. (Novato, CA: Presidio Press), 346.

[55] Ibid.

[56] Ibid.

[57] Megargee, *Inside Hitler's High Command*, 30.

[58] Forster, *Military Effectiveness Volume 3 The Second World War*, 202.

[59] Ibid., 200.

[60] *Document On German Foreign Policy 1918-1945, Series D 1937-1945 The War Years*, (Washington D.C.: United States Government Printing Office), Vol. XI, No. 21.

[61] Generaloberst Erhard Rauss, *Fighting in Hell, The German Ordeal On The Eastern Front.* Edited by Peter S. Tsouras. (New York, NY: Ivy Books), 147.

[62] Taylor and Shaw, *Dictionary of The Third Reich,* 265-266.

[63] Johnson, *A History of the Jews,* 495.

[64] Ibid., 505.

[65] William Shirer, *The Rise and Fall of The Third Reich.* (Greenwich, CT: Fawcett Publications, Inc.), 1125.

Glossary

Aryan: In National Socialist ideology a mythical Indo-European Race of Super Humans known in German as the Ubermenschen.

Blitzkrieg: Lightening War. A combined arms warfare technique.

Freikorps: Volunteer units.

Führerprinzip: Leadership Principle.

Lebensraum: Living Space.

Mein Kampf: My Struggle. Adolf Hitler's political treatise written in 1924 while in Landsberg Prison after the attempted 1923 Munich Putsch.

NSDAP - Nationalsozialistische Deutsche Arbeitspartei: The National Socialist German Workers Party.

Oberkommando der Wehrmacht (OKW): Armed Forces High Command

Oberkommando der Heeres (OKH): Army High Command

Schutzstaffel (SS): Security Squad or Defense Unit.

Sturmabteilung (SA): Storm Troopers. Party uniformed protection organization for party meetings, speeches, rallies, etc. known as the brown shirts. The SA was formed and led by WWI veteran Ernst Röhm.

Third Reich: Third Empire. First Empire being the Holy Roman Empire and the Second Empire established in 1871 after the Franco-Prussian War.

Untermenschen: Sub-humans. Inferior humans. This group included Gypsies, Jews, and Slavic peoples.

Vernichtungskrieg: A War of Annihilation

Völkisch: Of the People. The use of the German word völk for "people" in the nationalist context vice other acceptable terms for people is a racial construct that is meant to exclude those not ethnically German.

Volksgemeinschaft: People's community.

Volksstaat: Popular state.

Volkstumskampf: Ethnic struggle

Wehrmacht: Armed Forces. In National Socialist Germany the principle armed forces were the Army, Navy, Air Force, and the Armed SS (Waffen-SS).

Weltanschauung: Philosophy or World View.

Bibliography

Ayçoberry, Pierre. *The Social History of the Third Reich 1933-1945.* Translated from French by Janet Lloyd. New York, NY: The New Press, 1999.

Aspects of the Third Reich. Edited by H.W. Koch. Hong Kong: MacMillan, 1985.

Baxter, Ian. *SS: The Secret Archives, Eastern Front.* London, England: Amber Brooks Ltd, 2003.

Clausewitz, Carl von. *On War.* Edited by Michael Howard and Peter Paret. Translated by Michael Howard and Peter Paret. Princeton, NJ: Princeton University Press, 1984.

Corum, James S. *The Roots of Blitzkrieg, Hans von Seeckt and German Military Reform.* Lawrence, KS: United Press of Kansas, 1992.

DiNardo, Richard L. *Germany and the Axis Powers, From Coalition to Collapse.* Lawrence, KS: University Press of Kansas, 2005.

DiNardo, Richard L. *Mechanized Juggernaut or Military Anachronism? Horses and the German Army in WWII.* Mechanicsburg, PA: Stackpole Books, 2008.

Document On German Foreign Policy 1918-1945, Series D (1937-1945), Volume XI The War Years September 1, 1940- January 31, 1941. Board of Editors; United States: Howard M. Smyth, Editor-in-Chief; Arthur G. Kogan; George O. Kent; James Stuart Beddie. Great Britain: The Hon. Margaret Lambert, Editor-in-Chief; K.H.M. Duke; F.G. Stambrook; D.C. Watt; C.M. Breuning. France: Maurice Baumont, Editor-in-Chief; Georges Bonnin; André Scherer; Jacques Bariéty. Washington D.C.: United States Government Printing Office, 1960.*

Document On German Foreign Policy 1918-1945, Series D (1937-1945), Volume XII The War Years February 1- June 22, 1941. Board of Editors; United States: Howard M. Smyth, Editor-in-Chief; Arthur G. Kogan; George O. Kent; James Stuart Beddie. Great Britain: The Hon. Margaret Lambert, Editor-in-Chief; K.H.M. Duke; F.G. Stambrook; D.C. Watt; C.M. Breuning. France: Maurice Baumont, Editor-in-Chief; Georges Bonnin; André Scherer; Jacques Bariéty. Washington D.C.: United States Government Printing Office, 1962.

Germany and the Second World War: Volume IV The Attack on the Soviet Union. Edited by the Militärgeschichtliches Forschungsamt (Research Institute for Military History) Potsdam, Germany. Translated by Dean S. McMurry, Ewald Osers, and Louise Willmot. New York, NY: Oxford University Press, 1998.

Goldensohn, Leon. *The Nuremburg Interviews An American Psychiatrist's Conversation with the Defendants and Witnesses.* Edited by Robert Gellately. New York, NY: Vintage Books A Division of Random House, Inc., 2004.

Gray, Colin. "Defining and Achieving Decisive Victory." *Strategic Studies Institute Carlisle Barracks*, (April 2002): 1-52. http://www.carlisle.army.mil/usassi/erap.pdf

Grossjohann, Georg. *Five Years, Four Fronts, A German Officer's World War II Combat Memoir*. Translated by Ulrich Abele. New York, NY: Presidio Press, 2005.

Guderian, Heinz Wilhelm. *Achtung – Panzer!* Translated by Christopher Duffy. Introduction and Notes by Paul Harris. New York, NY: Arms and Armour Press, 1999.

Guderian, Heinz Wilhelm. *Panzer Leader*. New Introduction by Kenneth Macksey. Forward by B.H. Liddell Hart. Translated by Constantine Fitzgibbon. New York, NY: Da Capo Press, 1996.

Halder, Franz. *The Halder War Diary 1939-1942.* Abridged edition of the English translation of: Kriegstagebuch. Edited by Charles Burdick and Hans-Adolf Jacobsen. Novato, CA: Presidio Press, 1988.

Hart, B.H. Liddell. *History of the Second World War*. Old Saybrook, CT.: Konecky & Konecky, 1970.

Hart, B.H. Liddell. *The German Generals Talk*. New York, NY: Harper Perennial, 1948.

Hart, B.H. Liddell. *Strategy, Second Revised Edition*. New York, NY: A Meridian Book, 1991.

Hitler, Adolf. *Hitler's Second Book*. Edited by Gerhard L. Weinberg. Translated by Krista Smith. New York, NY: Enigma Books, 2003.

Hitler, Adolf. *Mein Kampf.* Translated by Ralph Manheim. Boston, Mass: Houghton Mifflin Company, 1971.

Hitler's Table Talk 1941-1944 His Private Conversations. Translated by Norman Cameron and R.H. Stevens. Introduced and with a new Preface by H.R. Trevor-Roper. New York, NY: Enigma Books, 2000.

Huntington, Samuel. *The Clash of Civilization and the Remaking of World Order*. New York, NY: Touchstone, 1997.

Jäckel, Eberhard. *Hitler's Weltanschauung: A Blueprint for Power.* Translated by Herbert Arnold. Middleton, Conn.: Wesleyan University Press, 1972.

Kelly, Justin. "Alien: How Operational Art Devoured Strategy." Strategic Studies Institute Carlisle Barracks, (September 2009): 11-85. http://www.StrategicStudiesInstitute.army.mil

Kershaw, Ian. *Hitler 1889-1936 Hubris.* New York, NY: W.W. Norton and Company, 2000.

Johnson, Paul. *A History of the Jews*. New York, NY: Harper and Row Publishers, 1987.

Kennedy, Paul. *The Rise and Fall of the Great Powers*. New York, NY: First Vintage Books, 1989.

Macksey, Kenneth. *Kesselring, The Making of the Luftwaffe. New York, NY: David McKay Company Inc., 1978.*

Magenheimer, Heinz. *Hitler's War, Germany's Key Strategic Decisions 1940-1945.* Translated by Helmut Bögler. New York, NY: Barnes and Noble Books, 2003.

Makers of Modern Strategy from Machiavelli to the Nuclear Age. Edited by Peter Paret. Princeton, NJ: Princeton University Press, 1986.

Military Effectiveness Volume 3 The Second World War, New Edition . Edited by Allan R. Millett and Williamson Murray. New York, NY: Cambridge University Press, 2010.

Megargee, Geoffrey P. *Inside Hitler's High Command.* Lawrence, KS: United Press of Kansas, 2000.

Merriam-Webster.com, "An Encyclopedia Britannica Company Merriam-Webster." Last modified 2012. Accessed October 23, 2012. http://www.merriam-webster.com/dictionary/ideology.

Murray, Williamson. Introduction to *Army Transformation: A View From the U.S. Army War College*, edited by Williamson Murray, 1-25. Strategic Studies Institute Carlisle Barracks, PN: U.S. Army War College, 2001.

Papen, Franz von. *Franz von Papen Memoirs.* Translated by Brian Connell. New York, NY: E.P. Dutton & Company Inc., 1953.

Rempel, Gerhard. *Hitler's Children: The Hitler Youth and the SS.* Chapel Hill, NC: The University of North Carolina Press, 1989.

Roberts, Andrew. *The Storm of War, A New History of the Second World War.* New York, NY: HarperCollins Publishers, 2011.

Rossino, Alexander B. *Blitzkrieg, Ideology, and Atrocity: Hitler Strikes Poland.* Lawrence, KS: University Press of Kansas, 2003.

Shepherd, Ben. *War in the Wild East, The German Army and Soviet Partisans.* Cambridge, MS: Harvard University Press, 2004.

Shirer, William. *The Rise and Fall of The Third Reich.* Greenwich, CT: Fawcett Publications, Inc., 1959.

Smith, Mark. *Operation Barbarossa June 22 to December 5, 1941.*Unbublished Marine Corps Command and Staff Campaign Study, 2012.

Snyder, Timothy. *Bloodlands, Europe Between Hitler and Stalin.* New York, NY: Basic Books, 2012.

Spielvogel, Jackson J. Second Edition, *Hitler and NAZI Germany, A History.* Englewood Cliffs, NJ: Simon & Shuster Company, 1992.

Speer, Albert. *Inside the Third Reich* Translated by Richard and Clara Winston, Introduced by Eugene Davidson. New York and Toronto: Macmillan, 1970.

Stern, Fritz. *The Politics of Cultural Despair: A Study in the Rise off the Germanic Ideology.* Berkeley and Los Angeles, CA: University of California Press, Ltd., 1989.

Taylor, James and Shaw, Warren. *Dictionary of The Third Reich.* New York, NY: Penguin Books, 1997.

Toland, John. *Adolf Hitler.* New York, NY: Ballantine Books, 1976.

Weale, Adrian. *Army of Evil, A History Of The SS.* New York, NY: New American Library, 2012.

Weinberg, Gerhard L. *A World At Arms, A Global History of World War II*, Second Edition. Cambridge, MA: Cambridge University Press, 2005.

Weinberg, Gerhard L. *The Foreign Policy of Hitler's Germany Starting World War II 1937-1939.* Chicago, IL: The University of Chicago Press, 1980.

Weiss, John. *Ideology of Death: Why The Holocaust Happened In Germany.* Chicago, IL: Elephant Paperbacks, 1997.

Williamson, Murray and Millett, Allen R., "Armored Warfare: The British, French and German Experiences," in *Military Innovation in the Interwar Period*, eds. Williamson Murray and Allan R. Millett (Cambridge: Cambridge University Press, 1996), 6-49.

World-wide German Dictionary. Compiled by Paul H. Glucksman. Edited by Herbert Rodeck and T.C. Appelt. New York, NY: Fawcett Premier, 1961.